The Sound of Silence: Breaking the Cycle of Workplace Gossip

Antoinette Kleinhans

The Sound of Silence: Breaking the Cycle of Workplace Gossip

Chapter 1: Understanding Workplace Gossip

Defining Gossip in the Workplace

Gossip in the workplace is often perceived as a trivial matter, yet it holds significant weight in shaping the culture of an organization. At its core, gossip can be defined as informal communication about individuals or situations that may or may not be true. This type of dialogue can manifest in various forms, from casual conversations by the water cooler to more structured discussions in meetings. Understanding what constitutes gossip is essential for recognizing its potential impact on team dynamics and overall workplace morale.

The nuances of workplace gossip extend beyond mere chatter; they encompass the motivations behind the sharing of information. Employees may engage in gossip for various reasons, such as seeking connection, gaining information, or even venting frustrations. While some gossip might seem harmless, it can quickly spiral into negativity when it involves spreading rumors or making assumptions about colleagues. Acknowledging these underlying motivations allows organizations to address the root causes of gossip and foster a more transparent and supportive environment.

The effects of gossip on morale and productivity cannot be understated. When gossip runs rampant, it can create an atmosphere of distrust and anxiety among employees. Individuals may feel they are being judged or scrutinized, leading to decreased job satisfaction and increased stress. This decline in morale can hinder collaboration, innovation, and overall productivity. Recognizing the detrimental effects of gossip is crucial for leaders aiming to cultivate a positive workplace culture that encourages open communication and teamwork.

However, it is important to note that not all gossip is inherently negative. In some cases, sharing information can facilitate bonding among team members and create a sense of community. When managed effectively, gossip can serve as a tool for connection, allowing employees to engage with one another and share their experiences. By channeling gossip into constructive conversations, organizations can promote camaraderie and strengthen relationships, ultimately enhancing workplace morale.

To break the cycle of negative gossip, organizations must prioritize open dialogue and establish clear communication channels. Encouraging employees to voice their concerns and share feedback in a safe environment can help mitigate misunderstandings and reduce the impulse to gossip. By fostering a culture of transparency and respect, workplaces can transform gossip from a source of division into a means of building unity and collaboration. With intentional effort, organizations can create a thriving atmosphere where employees feel valued and motivated, paving the way for greater productivity and success.

The Different Types of Gossip

The Sound of Silence: Breaking the Cycle of Workplace Gossip

Gossip in the workplace can be categorized into several types, each with its unique characteristics and impacts on the environment. Understanding these distinctions is critical for fostering a healthier workplace culture. The first type is benign gossip, which often involves light-hearted sharing of information or harmless chit-chat. This form of gossip can help build camaraderie among colleagues, creating bonds and enhancing team spirit. When employees engage in positive gossip, they reinforce relationships that can lead to improved collaboration and a more enjoyable work atmosphere.

Another type of gossip is evaluative gossip, which involves sharing opinions or judgments about coworkers. While this may seem harmless at first, evaluative gossip can quickly turn negative, leading to misunderstandings and strained relationships. It is essential to recognize the thin line between harmless evaluations and detrimental ones. Promoting open communication can help mitigate the risks of evaluative gossip, allowing employees to express their thoughts constructively rather than resorting to back-channel discussions that can harm morale and productivity.

In contrast, malicious gossip can be particularly damaging. This type involves spreading rumors, lies, or negative information about others with the intent to harm their reputation. Malicious gossip creates a toxic workplace environment, leading to distrust and fear among employees. It can significantly decrease morale, as individuals feel uncertain about their colleagues' intentions. Combating this type of gossip requires strong leadership and a commitment to fostering a culture of respect and accountability, where employees feel safe to address their concerns directly rather than through whispers.

There is also strategic gossip, which is often used as a tool for manipulation. Employees may share information selectively to gain an advantage or undermine others. This form of gossip can create divisions within teams and lead to a competitive, rather than collaborative, atmosphere. To counteract strategic gossip, organizations must promote transparency and encourage teamwork. By fostering an environment in which sharing information is viewed positively, employees will be less inclined to use gossip as a weapon against one another.

Lastly, there is social gossip, which focuses on general discussions about events, activities, or shared experiences. This type is generally more neutral and can serve as a bonding mechanism among employees. When managed well, social gossip can enhance workplace relationships and promote a sense of belonging. Encouraging employees to engage in positive social interactions can lead to a more cohesive and supportive work environment, ultimately boosting morale and productivity. By recognizing and addressing the various types of gossip, organizations can take proactive steps toward breaking the cycle and nurturing a healthier workplace culture.

The Psychological Triggers of Gossip

Gossip is a natural human behavior, deeply rooted in our social dynamics. It often arises from our intrinsic need to connect with others, share experiences, and seek validation. In the workplace, these conversations can serve as a double-edged sword, fostering camaraderie among colleagues while simultaneously breeding distrust and anxiety. Understanding the psychological triggers behind gossip can empower individuals and organizations to cultivate a more positive environment, enhancing both morale and productivity.

The Sound of Silence: Breaking the Cycle of Workplace Gossip

One key psychological trigger of gossip is the need for social bonding. When employees engage in gossip, they often do so to strengthen their relationships with one another. Sharing information, even if it is speculative or unverified, can create a sense of belonging and solidarity within a group. This social exchange can be beneficial when it promotes teamwork and collaboration, but it can also lead to cliques and exclusion if not managed appropriately. Encouraging open communication and transparency can help redirect this need for connection into more constructive channels, fostering an inclusive workplace culture.

Another significant factor is the desire for power and status. Gossip can be a way for individuals to assert their influence, positioning themselves as "in the know" or as someone who holds valuable information. This quest for status can lead to harmful behavior, as employees may exaggerate or distort facts to elevate their own standing. Organizations can mitigate this by promoting a culture of recognition that celebrates teamwork and collective successes rather than individual gossip-driven accolades. By valuing contributions based on merit and collaboration, workplaces can diminish the allure of gossip as a means of power.

Insecurity often fuels gossip as well. Employees may engage in gossip to alleviate their own feelings of inadequacy or fear of being judged. By discussing others, they can momentarily distract from their self-doubts and feel a sense of control over their environment. Addressing this insecurity through supportive mentorship and professional development can help individuals gain confidence in their roles. When employees feel valued and secure, they are less likely to resort to gossip as a coping mechanism, leading to a healthier workplace atmosphere.

Finally, the need for information plays a crucial role in the dynamics of workplace gossip. In environments where communication is limited or unclear, employees may turn to gossip as a source of information about decisions, changes, or policies affecting their work. This behavior is often exacerbated during times of uncertainty. To combat this, organizations should prioritize clear and consistent communication strategies. By ensuring that employees are well-informed and involved in the decision-making processes, companies can reduce the desire for gossip, fostering transparency and trust within the team.

Chapter 2: The Impact of Gossip on Morale

How Gossip Erodes Trust

Gossip in the workplace can create a toxic environment that erodes trust among team members. When rumors circulate, they often lead to misunderstandings and misinterpretations of intentions. This breakdown in communication can foster an atmosphere of suspicion, where employees feel they cannot rely on one another. Trust is the foundation of any successful team, and when it is diminished by gossip, the collaborative spirit that drives productivity and morale often suffers. By understanding the impact of gossip, we can take proactive steps to cultivate a more supportive workplace culture.

The Sound of Silence: Breaking the Cycle of Workplace Gossip

The cycle of gossip begins with a seemingly innocent comment or observation, which can quickly spiral into a damaging narrative. As information spreads, it is frequently distorted, leading to a cascading effect that can alienate individuals and create factions within a team. Colleagues may begin to second-guess each other's motives, undermining their ability to work together effectively. When trust is compromised, employees may become less willing to share ideas or seek help from one another, stifling creativity and innovation. Recognizing the subtle ways gossip can infiltrate the workplace is vital for fostering an environment where collaboration thrives.

Moreover, gossip can lead to decreased morale among employees. When people feel their contributions are scrutinized or misrepresented, it can result in disengagement and a lack of motivation. Employees may start to feel they are working in a hostile environment, which can affect their overall job satisfaction and commitment to the organization. It is crucial for leaders and team members to create an atmosphere where open communication is encouraged, allowing individuals to express their concerns in a constructive manner. By addressing the underlying issues that give rise to gossip, teams can work towards a more positive and inclusive workplace culture.

Building trust requires intentional effort and transparency. Organizations can implement strategies to combat gossip, such as encouraging regular team check-ins and fostering a culture of feedback. When team members feel safe to voice their thoughts and concerns, they are less likely to engage in gossip. Additionally, providing training on effective communication can help employees understand the value of sharing information directly and respectfully, rather than relying on hearsay. Encouraging a culture of respect and understanding can empower employees to rise above gossip and work collaboratively towards common goals.

Ultimately, breaking the cycle of gossip is a collective responsibility. Every employee has a role to play in creating a trustworthy environment. By choosing to approach conversations with kindness and integrity, individuals can contribute to a healthier workplace culture. It is essential for everyone to recognize the power of their words and the impact they can have on their colleagues. Together, we can foster an environment where trust flourishes, productivity soars, and employees feel valued and supported, leading to greater success for the entire organization.

The Ripple Effects on Team Dynamics

In any workplace, the dynamics of a team can be profoundly influenced by the presence of gossip. While it might seem harmless at first glance, gossip creates an environment that fosters distrust and negativity. When team members engage in gossip, it disrupts communication and can lead to misunderstandings. As a result, collaboration suffers, making it challenging for teams to work cohesively toward common goals. Recognizing the impact of gossip on team dynamics is crucial for fostering a healthier workplace culture.

The ripple effects of gossip extend beyond individual relationships and can alter the entire team atmosphere. When gossip circulates, it often results in feelings of anxiety and uncertainty among employees. This emotional turmoil can lead to decreased morale, as employees may feel alienated or targeted by unverified rumors. Consequently, team members may withdraw from open communication, fearing that their words could be misrepresented. By addressing and mitigating gossip, teams can nurture a more supportive environment where trust and respect flourish.

The Sound of Silence: Breaking the Cycle of Workplace Gossip

Moreover, gossip can significantly hinder productivity. When employees are preoccupied with rumors, their focus shifts away from their work responsibilities. Time that could be spent on collaboration or completing tasks is instead consumed by speculation and concern over personal relationships. By fostering a culture of transparency and encouraging direct communication, teams can redirect their energy toward achieving collective objectives rather than getting caught up in the negative spiral of gossip. This shift not only enhances productivity but also reinforces a sense of shared purpose.

Encouraging open dialogue within teams can also counteract the negative effects of gossip. When team members feel empowered to express their thoughts and concerns respectfully, it cultivates an environment of accountability. Regular check-ins and team-building activities can build understanding and strengthen bonds among colleagues, making it less likely for gossip to take root. By prioritizing communication, teams can create a space where individuals feel valued and heard, ultimately leading to a more harmonious work atmosphere.

In summary, the impact of gossip on team dynamics is profound, but it can be effectively managed. By fostering an environment of trust, encouraging open communication, and emphasizing collaboration, teams can mitigate the detrimental effects of gossip. Each member plays a vital role in shaping the workplace culture, and by committing to a more positive, inclusive approach, teams can thrive. Embracing this journey not only enhances morale and productivity but also paves the way for lasting relationships built on respect and understanding.

Recognizing the Signs of Low Morale

Low morale in the workplace can manifest in various subtle yet telling signs that, when recognized early, can lead to effective interventions and a revitalized work environment. One of the most common indicators is a noticeable decline in enthusiasm among employees. When team members who once displayed eagerness and passion for their work begin to show apathy or disengagement, it becomes crucial to take notice. This shift often signals that employees may feel undervalued or unsupported, prompting a need for open communication and reassurance from leadership.

Another sign of low morale is increased absenteeism or tardiness. When employees start to frequently miss work or arrive late, it can reflect a lack of motivation or a desire to avoid a negative atmosphere. This behavior not only affects productivity but can also spread feelings of discontent among remaining team members. Addressing these patterns with empathy and understanding can help to uncover underlying issues and re-establish a sense of belonging within the team.

Additionally, a rise in negative interactions among colleagues can be a clear signal of declining morale. Increased gossip, conflicts, or a general sense of hostility can create a toxic work environment that stifles collaboration and innovation. Recognizing these dynamics is essential for fostering a positive workplace culture. By promoting open dialogue and encouraging constructive feedback, leaders can help to mitigate these tensions and rebuild trust among team members.

The Sound of Silence: Breaking the Cycle of Workplace Gossip

A lack of initiative or creativity in problem-solving can also indicate low morale. When employees no longer feel inspired to contribute ideas or take ownership of their work, it signals a critical need for revitalization. Encouraging team members to share their thoughts and recognizing their contributions can reignite their passion and commitment to their roles. Providing opportunities for professional development and encouraging a growth mindset can further enhance engagement and satisfaction.

Lastly, paying attention to the overall emotional climate of the workplace is vital. If employees appear consistently stressed, anxious, or withdrawn, it is essential to address these feelings proactively. Creating a supportive environment where employees feel safe to express their concerns can lead to significant improvements in morale. By recognizing these signs and fostering an atmosphere of openness and support, organizations can break the cycle of negativity and build a thriving, productive workplace where everyone feels valued and motivated to contribute.

Chapter 3: The Consequences for Productivity

Distraction and Loss of Focus

Distraction and loss of focus are significant challenges that many employees face in today's fast-paced work environment. In a workplace rife with gossip, these distractions can become even more pronounced, undermining both morale and productivity. When conversations drift toward rumors and speculation, they pull attention away from essential tasks, leading to a sense of disconnection among team members. Recognizing the impact of these distractions is the first step toward fostering a more focused and harmonious workplace.

The nature of gossip often creates an atmosphere of uncertainty and anxiety. Employees may feel compelled to engage in or listen to gossip, fearing they might miss out on critical information or social dynamics. This preoccupation can erode concentration, making it challenging for individuals to complete their work efficiently. By addressing the root causes of gossip and promoting open communication, organizations can help employees regain their focus and invest their energies in productive activities that benefit both themselves and their teams.

Moreover, when employees are distracted by gossip, the overall morale of the workplace can suffer. A culture that tolerates or encourages gossip fosters an environment of distrust and negativity. Employees may feel less inclined to collaborate or share ideas, fearing that their contributions will be misinterpreted or used against them. By actively discouraging gossip and promoting a culture of respect and transparency, leaders can create a more supportive environment that encourages individuals to focus on their work and personal growth.

Additionally, the cycle of gossip can lead to a significant decline in productivity. Time spent engaging in or listening to gossip is time taken away from achieving goals and meeting deadlines. Teams that are constantly distracted by rumors are less likely to perform at their best. Encouraging employees to redirect their attention toward constructive conversations and team-building activities can help break this cycle. When employees feel empowered to communicate openly and positively, the overall productivity of the organization can flourish.

The Sound of Silence: Breaking the Cycle of Workplace Gossip

Ultimately, overcoming distraction and loss of focus caused by workplace gossip requires commitment from both leaders and employees. By fostering an environment where open dialogue is encouraged, and gossip is actively discouraged, organizations can create a culture that values focus and productivity. This transformation not only enhances individual performance but also strengthens team cohesion and morale. Embracing the sound of silence in the workplace can lead to a more engaged workforce, one that thrives on collaboration and shared success.

The Cost of High Turnover Rates

High turnover rates can be a significant challenge for organizations, often leading to a cascade of negative effects that extend beyond the immediate loss of employees. Each departure can disrupt team dynamics, erode trust, and create a sense of instability within the workplace. When employees frequently leave, remaining staff may feel overworked and undervalued, leading to low morale. This shift in atmosphere can foster a breeding ground for workplace gossip, as employees search for someone or something to blame for their dissatisfaction.

The financial implications of high turnover are also considerable. Organizations invest substantial resources in recruiting, hiring, and training new employees. When turnover occurs, these investments can quickly become wasted efforts, leading to increased costs that can strain budgets. Moreover, the time spent onboarding new hires detracts from the productivity of existing staff, who may have to take on extra responsibilities in the interim. This cycle not only impacts the bottom line but also detracts from the overall effectiveness of the team.

Furthermore, high turnover rates can hinder the development of a cohesive workplace culture. When employees do not stay long enough to build relationships and understand the organization's values, it becomes challenging to create a sense of belonging. This lack of connection can amplify feelings of isolation among team members, increasing the likelihood of gossip as individuals seek to vent their frustrations. A harmonious work environment thrives on strong relationships, and turnover disrupts this essential foundation.

However, organizations can take proactive steps to mitigate the effects of high turnover. By fostering open communication, offering opportunities for professional growth, and recognizing employee contributions, businesses can create a more supportive atmosphere. This positive environment not only decreases the likelihood of gossip but also encourages employees to remain committed to the organization. When employees feel valued and engaged, they are less likely to leave, ultimately contributing to a more stable and productive workforce.

In conclusion, while high turnover rates pose significant challenges, they also present an opportunity for organizations to reflect on their workplace culture and practices. By understanding the costs associated with turnover and taking deliberate action to address underlying issues, businesses can cultivate a positive environment that discourages gossip and fosters collaboration. Emphasizing employee satisfaction and engagement not only benefits individuals but strengthens the organization as a whole, paving the way for sustained success and a vibrant workplace culture.

Case Studies: Companies Affected by Gossip

The Sound of Silence: Breaking the Cycle of Workplace Gossip

In the realm of workplace dynamics, gossip can have a profound impact on organizational culture and employee morale. Consider Company X, a mid-sized tech firm that once thrived on innovation and collaboration. As rumors began to circulate about potential layoffs, the atmosphere shifted dramatically. Employees who once collaborated openly became guarded and secretive. Productivity took a hit as teams became preoccupied with speculation rather than focusing on their projects. However, the leadership recognized the detrimental effects of gossip and took proactive steps to address the issue. They initiated open forums where employees could express their concerns and receive transparent updates about the company's direction, ultimately fostering a culture of trust and engagement.

Another illustrative case is Company Y, a retail giant that faced a significant backlash due to gossip about favoritism within management. Employees began to feel alienated and demotivated, believing that their hard work went unnoticed while others were elevated without merit. The leadership team took the situation seriously, implementing a merit-based recognition program that highlighted the achievements of all employees. By amplifying the voices of their workforce and showcasing the hard work of individuals across all levels, Company Y not only mitigated the effects of gossip but also revitalized employee morale, leading to improved productivity and a more cohesive work environment.

In contrast, Company Z, a startup known for its vibrant culture, experienced a decline in team cohesion due to rampant gossip concerning leadership decisions. The lack of clarity around strategic choices led to confusion and a sense of disillusionment among employees. Recognizing the urgent need for change, the founders introduced regular town hall meetings to discuss company strategies and to invite feedback from employees. This initiative not only dispelled the rumors but also empowered employees to engage in constructive dialogue, ultimately reinforcing a sense of community and shared purpose within the organization.

A notable example of overcoming gossip can be seen in Company A, a healthcare provider that faced damaging rumors about its financial stability. Employees were anxious, leading to decreased focus on patient care. The management team decided to confront the issue head-on by providing regular financial updates and emphasizing the organization's commitment to its mission. This transparency not only quelled the gossip but also re-energized the staff, who felt more connected to the organization's goals. The result was a renewed sense of pride in their work, demonstrating that addressing gossip directly can pave the way for a more positive workplace culture.

Lastly, Company B, a manufacturing firm, serves as a reminder of the potential long-term effects of unchecked gossip. When a rumor about a significant merger began to circulate, it created division among employees, with some feeling secure and others fearing job loss. The management recognized the need for intervention and organized workshops focused on building communication skills and fostering a supportive environment. By encouraging open dialogue and promoting understanding, Company B not only quelled the gossip but also cultivated a more resilient workforce. This case illustrates that while gossip can create challenges, it also presents an opportunity for growth and improvement, ultimately leading to a stronger, more united organization.

The Sound of Silence: Breaking the Cycle of Workplace Gossip

Chapter 4: The Role of Leadership in Addressing Gossip

Setting the Right Tone from the Top

Setting the right tone from the top is crucial in fostering a positive workplace culture that actively combats gossip. Leaders set the example for their teams, influencing the dynamics of communication and interaction within the organization. When leadership embodies transparency, respect, and open dialogue, it creates an environment where employees feel valued and safe. This, in turn, lays the groundwork for a culture that discourages gossip and promotes constructive conversations.

Leaders can begin by openly discussing the negative impacts of gossip on morale and productivity. Holding regular meetings where these issues are addressed not only shows that leadership is aware of the problem but also encourages employees to share their experiences. This creates a platform for open communication, allowing team members to voice their concerns without fear of judgment. By fostering this dialogue, leaders can demystify misunderstandings and prevent the spread of unchecked rumors, ultimately strengthening the team's cohesion.

Moreover, leaders should model the behavior they wish to see in their teams. This means demonstrating effective communication skills, practicing active listening, and engaging in respectful conflict resolution. When leaders approach disagreements or discussions with a focus on collaboration rather than competition, it shifts the narrative from gossip to problem-solving. Employees are more likely to follow suit, recognizing that they can address issues constructively rather than resorting to hearsay.

Recognition and appreciation play pivotal roles in setting the right tone. Leaders should celebrate individual and team successes publicly, reinforcing positive behavior and encouraging employees to support one another. This not only boosts morale but also creates a sense of belonging and teamwork. When employees feel recognized for their contributions, they are less likely to engage in gossip and more inclined to uplift their colleagues, fostering a supportive environment.

Finally, establishing clear policies and expectations regarding workplace communication can further reinforce a gossip-free culture. Leaders should articulate the importance of respectful communication and outline the consequences of spreading rumors. By having these guidelines in place, employees understand that their actions have implications, encouraging them to think twice before engaging in gossip. When leaders consistently uphold these standards, it solidifies a tone of respect and accountability, creating a workplace where positive interactions thrive.

Encouraging Open Communication

The Sound of Silence: Breaking the Cycle of Workplace Gossip

Encouraging open communication in the workplace is essential for creating a positive and productive environment. When employees feel comfortable sharing their thoughts, concerns, and ideas, it fosters a sense of belonging and collaboration. This open dialogue not only strengthens relationships among team members but also helps to alleviate the negative impacts of gossip. By promoting transparency, organizations can cultivate a culture where employees feel valued and heard, reducing the likelihood of misunderstandings that often fuel workplace gossip.

One effective way to encourage open communication is to establish regular check-ins and feedback sessions. These meetings provide a structured opportunity for employees to voice their opinions and discuss any challenges they may be facing. Encouraging managers to actively listen during these sessions can help employees feel more at ease. When team members see that their input is taken seriously and acted upon, they are more likely to engage in honest discussions, ultimately leading to a more cohesive work environment.

Another important aspect of fostering open communication is creating safe spaces for dialogue. Organizations can implement anonymous feedback tools or suggestion boxes, allowing employees to express their concerns without fear of retribution. This anonymity can be particularly helpful in addressing sensitive topics that may otherwise be left unspoken. By ensuring that all voices are heard, companies can not only reduce the prevalence of gossip but also gain valuable insights into areas for improvement and growth.

Training and development programs can also play a pivotal role in encouraging open communication. Workshops focused on effective communication skills, active listening, and conflict resolution can empower employees to engage in healthy conversations. By equipping team members with the tools they need to communicate effectively, organizations can create an atmosphere where discussions are constructive rather than destructive. This proactive approach can significantly reduce the negative impact of gossip and enhance overall morale.

Finally, leadership plays a crucial role in modeling open communication. When leaders demonstrate transparency and vulnerability, it sets a powerful example for the rest of the team. By sharing their own challenges and encouraging discussions around them, leaders can help break down barriers and foster a culture of trust. When employees see that their leaders prioritize communication, they are more likely to mirror those behaviors, creating a workplace where everyone feels empowered to speak up and contribute positively to the organizational culture.

Developing a Gossip Policy

Developing a gossip policy is a crucial step toward fostering a healthier workplace environment. A well-crafted policy not only addresses the negative impact of gossip but also encourages open communication and trust among employees. By establishing clear guidelines, organizations can create a culture where employees feel safe discussing their concerns directly with one another rather than resorting to harmful gossip. This proactive approach can lead to improved morale and productivity, as employees are more likely to focus on their work when they feel respected and heard.

The Sound of Silence: Breaking the Cycle of Workplace Gossip

To begin developing an effective gossip policy, it is essential to involve employees in the process. By seeking input from various team members, organizations can gain valuable insights into the unique dynamics of their workplace. This collaboration not only promotes a sense of ownership but also helps identify specific gossip-related issues that may need addressing. When employees see their voices reflected in the policy, they are more likely to embrace it and work together to uphold its principles. This collective effort fosters unity, making it clear that everyone shares the responsibility of maintaining a positive work atmosphere.

Once employee input has been gathered, the next step is to define what constitutes gossip in the workplace. A clear definition will help employees understand the boundaries of acceptable communication. The policy should emphasize that while casual conversations are a natural part of workplace interactions, spreading unverified information or discussing colleagues in a negative light is harmful. By clarifying these distinctions, organizations can guide employees toward healthier communication practices, ultimately reducing the instances of gossip and its detrimental effects on morale and productivity.

Additionally, the gossip policy should outline the consequences of engaging in gossip and the processes for addressing any breaches. It is important for employees to understand that there will be accountability for negative behaviors, but also that the organization is committed to supporting those who come forward with concerns. This balance fosters a culture of transparency and respect. Encouraging employees to report incidents of gossip, whether they are direct victims or witnesses, can help address issues before they escalate and contribute to a more supportive workplace environment.

Finally, ongoing training and reinforcement of the gossip policy are vital to its success. Regular workshops or discussions can help keep the topic at the forefront of employees' minds, ensuring that the principles of the policy are actively practiced. Celebrating positive examples of communication and collaboration can also reinforce the desired behaviors. By continuously promoting a culture of respect and openness, organizations can effectively break the cycle of workplace gossip, leading to enhanced morale and productivity. A strong gossip policy, when developed and implemented thoughtfully, can transform the workplace into a space where everyone thrives.

Chapter 5: Creating a Positive Workplace Culture

The Importance of Team Building

Team building is an essential aspect of creating a healthy workplace environment, particularly in combating the negative effects of gossip. When individuals come together as a cohesive unit, they foster trust, open communication, and mutual respect. These elements are critical in breaking down the barriers that gossip creates. By engaging in team-building activities, employees not only enhance their interpersonal relationships but also develop a shared sense of purpose, which can significantly reduce the likelihood of gossip taking root in the workplace.

The Sound of Silence: Breaking the Cycle of Workplace Gossip

One of the most significant benefits of team building is the improvement in morale that it fosters. When employees feel connected to their colleagues, they are more likely to contribute positively to the workplace culture. Team-building exercises encourage collaboration and camaraderie, allowing individuals to appreciate each other's strengths and perspectives. This positive reinforcement can lead to increased job satisfaction, which directly counters the negativity that gossip often brings. As morale improves, employees are more inclined to support one another, creating an environment where gossip is less likely to thrive.

Moreover, team building enhances communication skills among employees. Effective communication is vital in preventing misunderstandings that often lead to gossip. Through team-building activities, employees learn to express their thoughts and feelings in constructive ways, fostering open dialogue. This open communication not only addresses potential issues before they escalate but also cultivates an atmosphere where employees feel safe discussing their concerns without fear of judgment or backlash. A workplace that prioritizes clear communication will find that gossip diminishes as employees feel heard and respected.

In addition to boosting morale and communication, team building contributes to increased productivity. When employees work well together, they can accomplish tasks more efficiently and effectively. A strong team dynamic allows for the pooling of diverse skills and ideas, leading to innovative solutions and improved performance. When employees are focused on collaborating rather than engaging in gossip, they can dedicate their energy towards achieving common goals. This shift in focus not only enhances individual performance but also propels the entire team toward success.

Ultimately, investing in team-building initiatives is a proactive approach to mitigating the impact of gossip in the workplace. By prioritizing the development of strong relationships, effective communication, and a positive work culture, organizations can create a foundation that discourages gossip and promotes collaboration. As employees bond over shared experiences and achievements, they cultivate a sense of belonging that is crucial for a thriving workplace. In doing so, they break the cycle of negativity and pave the way for a more harmonious and productive environment.

Fostering Inclusivity and Respect

Fostering an environment of inclusivity and respect is essential for breaking the cycle of workplace gossip. When employees feel valued and included, they are more likely to engage positively with their colleagues, leading to a healthier work atmosphere. This sense of belonging mitigates the harmful effects of gossip, as individuals are less inclined to engage in negative talk when they feel respected and appreciated. Organizations that actively promote inclusivity create a culture where employees can voice their opinions and ideas without fear of judgment, paving the way for open communication and collaboration.

One effective approach to fostering inclusivity is through team-building activities that celebrate diversity. By engaging employees in activities that highlight their unique backgrounds and perspectives, organizations can cultivate appreciation for differences. These experiences not only strengthen bonds among team members but also encourage understanding and empathy. When employees work together in an inclusive setting, they are less likely to partake in gossip and more likely to support one another, enhancing overall morale and productivity.

The Sound of Silence: Breaking the Cycle of Workplace Gossip

Encouraging open dialogue is another critical element in promoting respect within the workplace. Establishing platforms for employees to share their thoughts and concerns can significantly reduce the tendency for gossip to thrive. Regular feedback sessions, suggestion boxes, or open-door policies allow employees to express their feelings and experiences candidly. When individuals feel heard and acknowledged, they are less likely to resort to gossip as a means of expressing dissatisfaction or frustration, creating a more harmonious work environment.

Training programs focused on communication skills and conflict resolution can also play a vital role in fostering inclusivity. Equipping employees with the tools to navigate difficult conversations and misunderstandings can diminish the likelihood of gossip taking root. When team members are trained to address issues directly and constructively, they cultivate a sense of trust and respect among each other. This proactive approach not only enhances interpersonal relationships but also contributes to a more productive and cohesive workplace.

Ultimately, fostering inclusivity and respect requires a collective commitment from everyone within the organization. Leaders must model inclusive behavior, demonstrating the importance of treating all individuals with dignity. By prioritizing inclusivity, organizations can create a culture that celebrates diversity, encourages collaboration, and significantly reduces the prevalence of gossip. When employees feel respected and valued, they are empowered to contribute positively, leading to enhanced morale and improved productivity for the entire organization.

Celebrating Achievements and Successes

Celebrating achievements and successes is a vital aspect of fostering a positive work environment that counters the detrimental effects of workplace gossip. When team members actively recognize and appreciate each other's contributions, it creates a culture of support and motivation. This culture not only boosts morale but also enhances productivity, as individuals feel valued and engaged in their work. Acknowledging successes, whether big or small, encourages a shared sense of purpose and camaraderie among colleagues, ultimately leading to a more cohesive team.

Recognizing achievements can take many forms, from formal awards and accolades to simple verbal affirmations. The key is to ensure that recognition is frequent and sincere. By celebrating milestones, completed projects, or personal accomplishments, organizations can shift the focus away from negative narratives that often arise from gossip. When employees see their peers being celebrated, it fosters an environment where everyone feels encouraged to strive for excellence, knowing that their hard work will be acknowledged.

Moreover, celebrating successes can serve as a powerful antidote to the isolation that often comes with gossip. When individuals feel connected through shared celebrations, it creates an atmosphere of positivity and trust. Team-building activities, recognition events, or even casual gatherings to celebrate wins can help break down barriers and foster open communication. This sense of belonging not only diminishes the allure of gossip but also encourages individuals to support one another, reinforcing a collaborative spirit.

The Sound of Silence: Breaking the Cycle of Workplace Gossip

Leadership plays a crucial role in this celebration process. Leaders who prioritize recognition and celebrate team achievements set a profound example for their employees. By making it a point to acknowledge both individual and team successes during meetings or through internal communications, leaders can inspire a culture of appreciation. This leadership approach not only motivates employees but also signals that the organization values their contributions, further reducing the tendency for gossip to flourish.

In conclusion, celebrating achievements and successes is essential in breaking the cycle of workplace gossip. By creating an environment where individuals feel appreciated and recognized, organizations can enhance morale and productivity. When employees unite in celebration, they build stronger relationships and a supportive community that thrives on positivity rather than negativity. This shift not only enriches the workplace experience but also fosters a culture that actively discourages gossip, paving the way for a more harmonious and productive work environment.

Chapter 6: Strategies for Employees to Combat Gossip

How to Respond to Gossip Effectively

Responding to gossip effectively requires a thoughtful approach that can help maintain a positive work environment. First, it is essential to remain calm and composed when faced with gossip. Recognizing that gossip often stems from insecurity or misunderstanding can help you detach emotionally from the situation. By not reacting impulsively, you position yourself to respond in a way that fosters clarity and respect. Take a moment to breathe and assess the situation before engaging in any discussion, ensuring your response is measured and constructive.

When addressing gossip, consider the context in which it arises. Engaging with colleagues in a friendly and open manner can encourage a culture of transparency. If you hear rumors circulating about yourself or others, approach the sources directly and ask for clarification. This not only helps dispel the misinformation but also demonstrates your commitment to open communication. By confronting the issue head-on, you encourage others to adopt the same approach, creating an environment where gossip is less likely to flourish.

Another effective strategy is to shift the focus of conversation away from negative gossip. When you encounter gossip in discussions, gently redirect the conversation towards more productive topics. For instance, if colleagues are talking about someone's shortcomings, suggest discussing their recent achievements instead. This practice not only elevates the conversation but also reinforces a culture of recognition and support. By steering discussions towards positive contributions, you can help diminish the allure of gossip and promote an atmosphere of encouragement.

The Sound of Silence: Breaking the Cycle of Workplace Gossip

It's also crucial to set a personal example of integrity and respect in the workplace. By refraining from participating in gossip and demonstrating professionalism, you can inspire your peers to follow suit. Share positive stories, celebrate team successes, and highlight the strengths of your colleagues. When you model this behavior, you create a ripple effect that can gradually reduce the prevalence of gossip. Your actions will encourage others to communicate in ways that build up rather than tear down, fostering a more collaborative and harmonious work environment.

Finally, it is important to seek support if gossip persists and affects morale or productivity. Engaging with human resources or a trusted supervisor can provide additional strategies for addressing the issue. Building a supportive network can help you navigate challenging situations and reinforce the message that gossip is not acceptable. By uniting with others who share your commitment to respect and professionalism, you can create a stronger, more resilient workplace culture. Together, you can cultivate an environment where open communication flourishes, and gossip becomes a thing of the past.

Building Stronger Relationships with Colleagues

Building strong relationships with colleagues is essential for fostering a positive work environment and mitigating the adverse effects of workplace gossip. When team members cultivate mutual respect and understanding, they create a culture of openness that discourages negative talk. This foundation allows individuals to feel valued and appreciated, enhancing their sense of belonging within the team. As colleagues grow closer, they naturally become more supportive of one another, which can significantly reduce the likelihood of gossip taking root.

Effective communication is a cornerstone of strong professional relationships. Encouraging honest and transparent dialogue among team members can help clarify misunderstandings before they escalate into rumors. By actively listening to one another and providing constructive feedback, colleagues can create an atmosphere of trust. When individuals feel they can share their thoughts and concerns without fear of judgment, they are less likely to resort to gossip as a means of expressing frustration or discontent.

Collaboration plays a vital role in strengthening workplace relationships. By working together on projects or tasks, colleagues can build camaraderie and develop a sense of shared purpose. This collaborative spirit not only enhances productivity but also fosters deeper connections between team members. When colleagues celebrate each other's successes and support one another during challenges, they lay the groundwork for a more cohesive team dynamic that is resilient against the corrosive effects of gossip.

Investing time in social interactions can also significantly boost relationships among colleagues. Informal gatherings, team-building activities, and even casual conversations during breaks can break down barriers and encourage a more friendly atmosphere. These moments of connection can transform the workplace from a competitive environment into a supportive community where individuals feel encouraged to share their experiences and insights. As relationships deepen, colleagues are more likely to approach each other directly with concerns or grievances rather than resorting to gossip.

The Sound of Silence: Breaking the Cycle of Workplace Gossip

Ultimately, building stronger relationships with colleagues is a proactive approach to creating a healthier workplace culture. When individuals prioritize connection, communication, and collaboration, they not only enhance their own work experiences but also contribute to the overall morale and productivity of the team. By breaking the cycle of gossip and fostering genuine relationships, employees can create a workplace where everyone feels empowered, valued, and motivated to contribute their best efforts.

Encouraging Positive Conversations

Encouraging positive conversations in the workplace is essential for fostering a healthy and productive environment. When team members engage in uplifting discussions, it cultivates a sense of belonging and camaraderie. By focusing on constructive dialogue, employees can build trust and respect among one another, creating a foundation for collaboration. This, in turn, reduces the likelihood of gossip, which often thrives in atmospheres filled with negativity and misunderstandings.

To promote positive conversations, leaders should model the behavior they wish to see. Open communication is vital, and when managers actively listen to their employees, it encourages them to express their thoughts and concerns. Creating an open-door policy can help employees feel comfortable sharing their ideas and challenges without fear of judgment. This environment of transparency not only discourages gossip but also empowers employees to voice their opinions, leading to problem-solving and innovation.

Another effective strategy is to celebrate achievements, both big and small. Recognizing individual and team contributions fosters a culture of appreciation and positivity. When employees feel valued for their hard work, they are more likely to engage in uplifting conversations about their peers. This creates a ripple effect, as positivity spreads and employees become more inclined to support one another, enhancing overall morale and productivity.

Incorporating team-building activities is another excellent way to encourage positive conversations. These activities can break down barriers and cultivate relationships among colleagues. When people collaborate in a relaxed setting, they often discover shared interests and strengths, which can lead to more meaningful interactions in the workplace. As interpersonal connections deepen, the potential for gossip diminishes, replaced by supportive dialogues that enhance teamwork.

Finally, providing training on effective communication can equip employees with the skills they need to engage in positive conversations. Workshops that focus on active listening, empathy, and conflict resolution can transform the way team members interact. By arming employees with these tools, organizations can reduce the prevalence of gossip and create a culture where positive dialogue thrives. Ultimately, fostering an environment rich in constructive conversation not only boosts morale but also enhances productivity, leading to a more harmonious workplace.

Chapter 7: Tools for Managers to Foster Transparency

The Sound of Silence: Breaking the Cycle of Workplace Gossip

Implementing Feedback Mechanisms

Implementing feedback mechanisms is a crucial step in fostering a positive workplace culture and mitigating the adverse effects of gossip. By establishing clear channels for communication, organizations empower employees to voice their concerns and share constructive feedback. This proactive approach not only enhances morale but also strengthens relationships among team members. When employees feel heard, they are more likely to contribute positively to the workplace environment, diminishing the allure of gossip and fostering collaboration.

One effective method for implementing feedback mechanisms is through regular check-ins and one-on-one meetings. These sessions provide employees with a safe space to express their thoughts and feelings about their work environment. Leaders should approach these meetings with an open mind and a genuine desire to understand their team's perspectives. By showing that feedback is valued and taken seriously, organizations can create a culture of trust where employees feel comfortable discussing issues, including those related to gossip.

Another powerful tool is the establishment of anonymous feedback systems. These can take the form of surveys or suggestion boxes that allow employees to share their insights without fear of reprisal. This anonymity can encourage more honest and candid feedback, especially on sensitive topics like workplace gossip. When employees know their voices matter, they are more likely to engage in constructive conversations rather than resorting to negative talk behind each other's backs. As a result, the organization can address underlying issues before they escalate.

Training managers and team leaders on how to respond to feedback effectively can further enhance the impact of feedback mechanisms. When leaders model active listening and demonstrate that they are taking action based on employee input, it reinforces the importance of open communication. This approach not only builds trust but also demonstrates a commitment to resolving conflicts and improving workplace dynamics. Employees will feel more empowered to engage in positive interactions, reducing the frequency of gossip and enhancing overall productivity.

Finally, it is essential to celebrate the positive outcomes that arise from implementing feedback mechanisms. Recognizing improvements in team morale and productivity can motivate employees to continue sharing their thoughts and contributing to a healthy workplace culture. By highlighting success stories and acknowledging the collective efforts to overcome gossip, organizations can inspire a sense of belonging and commitment among their employees. This transformation from a gossip-prone environment to one where feedback is valued is not just beneficial; it is attainable and essential for long-term success.

Regular Check-Ins and Team Meetings

The Sound of Silence: Breaking the Cycle of Workplace Gossip

Regular check-ins and team meetings serve as vital tools in fostering a positive workplace environment and reducing the potential for gossip. When teams engage in consistent communication, it creates a culture of transparency and trust. Regularly scheduled meetings provide an opportunity for employees to voice their concerns, share updates, and discuss any issues that may be impacting their work. This open dialogue helps to eliminate misunderstandings and ensures that everyone is on the same page, diminishing the likelihood of rumors taking root.

During these gatherings, it's essential to create a safe space where team members feel comfortable expressing their thoughts and feelings. Encouragement from leadership to speak openly can help break down barriers and reduce the fear of judgment that often fuels gossip. By actively listening to each person's input and acknowledging their contributions, leaders can reinforce the importance of collaboration and mutual respect. This approach not only bolsters morale but also cultivates a sense of belonging among team members, which is crucial for maintaining high productivity levels.

In addition to addressing concerns, regular check-ins can be an excellent opportunity to celebrate achievements and recognize individual efforts. When employees feel valued and appreciated, they are less likely to engage in negative behaviors like gossip. Highlighting successes, whether big or small, fosters a positive atmosphere where team members are motivated to support one another. This shift in focus from competition to collaboration can significantly enhance overall team dynamics and further discourage the spread of harmful speculation.

It's also beneficial to incorporate structured feedback sessions into these meetings. Constructive feedback encourages growth and development, allowing team members to learn from one another. When employees receive guidance and support, they are more inclined to address their challenges directly rather than resorting to gossip as a means of coping. This proactive approach to communication not only enhances individual performance but also contributes to a more cohesive team environment, where everyone feels empowered to contribute positively.

Finally, establishing a routine for regular check-ins and team meetings reinforces the idea that communication is a priority. When employees see that their leaders are committed to open dialogue, they are more likely to emulate that behavior among themselves. This ripple effect can transform the workplace culture, reducing the prevalence of gossip and fostering a more supportive atmosphere. By prioritizing regular communication, organizations can build stronger teams, enhance morale, and ultimately improve productivity, creating a workplace where silence is no longer filled with whispers but rather with encouragement and collaboration.

Utilizing Technology to Promote Openness

In today's fast-paced work environment, technology plays a pivotal role in fostering openness and transparency among employees. By leveraging various digital tools, organizations can create an atmosphere where communication flows freely, reducing the likelihood of misunderstandings and gossip. Platforms such as instant messaging applications, collaborative workspaces, and video conferencing tools enable teams to connect in real time, fostering a culture of openness that encourages employees to share their thoughts and concerns openly. This proactive approach not only diminishes the chances of gossip but also aligns the team towards common goals, enhancing overall productivity.

The Sound of Silence: Breaking the Cycle of Workplace Gossip

Utilizing technology to promote openness begins with the implementation of communication platforms that facilitate direct dialogue. Tools like Slack or Microsoft Teams allow employees to engage in conversations without the barriers that traditional email may impose. This immediacy in communication helps to clarify issues and dispel rumors before they can gain traction. Moreover, these platforms often include channels dedicated to specific topics or projects, which can help keep discussions focused and relevant. By encouraging employees to voice their opinions and share updates, organizations can cultivate a sense of belonging and engagement, ultimately reducing negative gossip.

Another effective way technology can promote openness is through the use of anonymous feedback tools. Applications like SurveyMonkey or Google Forms enable employees to express their thoughts and concerns without fear of retribution. This anonymity can empower team members to share insights that they might otherwise hesitate to voice, especially regarding sensitive topics. By regularly soliciting feedback, management demonstrates a commitment to listening and addressing employee concerns, which can significantly enhance morale. When employees feel their voices are heard, they are less likely to engage in gossip, as they trust that their issues will be addressed constructively.

Video conferencing has also revolutionized how teams communicate, particularly in remote work scenarios. Platforms such as Zoom or Microsoft Teams provide a face-to-face interaction experience that can strengthen relationships among team members. Virtual meetings allow for real-time discussions, promoting transparency in decision-making processes and reducing the ambiguity that often breeds gossip. When employees can see and hear each other, it fosters a sense of connection and accountability, encouraging them to communicate openly and honestly rather than resorting to speculation or rumor.

Finally, integrating technology with workplace culture initiatives can amplify the efforts to promote openness. Organizations can utilize digital platforms to share success stories, highlight team achievements, and celebrate individual contributions. By showcasing positive outcomes and recognizing employee efforts, companies not only boost morale but also create an environment where open communication is valued and rewarded. This proactive acknowledgment helps to build trust among team members, reducing the likelihood of gossip and fostering a more collaborative and productive workplace overall. Embracing technology as a tool for openness can lead to a harmonious work environment where employees feel valued, engaged, and empowered.

Chapter 8: The Path Forward: Moving Beyond Gossip

Embracing a Culture of Kindness

The Sound of Silence: Breaking the Cycle of Workplace Gossip

Embracing a culture of kindness in the workplace is essential for fostering an environment where employees feel valued and respected. Kindness serves as a powerful antidote to the negativity that gossip can create. When team members actively practice kindness, they contribute to building trust and open communication. This creates a supportive atmosphere where individuals feel empowered to express their thoughts and ideas without fear of judgment or ridicule. By prioritizing kindness, organizations can cultivate a sense of belonging that enhances morale and promotes collaboration.

One of the most effective ways to instill a culture of kindness is through leadership. Leaders set the tone for the organization, and their commitment to kindness can inspire employees at all levels. When leaders demonstrate empathy, actively listen, and recognize the contributions of their team members, they model the behavior they wish to see. This ripple effect encourages others to adopt similar practices, creating a unified approach to interpersonal interactions. A workplace where kindness is modeled from the top down not only mitigates the harmful effects of gossip but also enhances overall workplace satisfaction.

In addition to leadership, organizations can implement initiatives that promote kindness among employees. Simple acts, such as recognizing a colleague's achievements or encouraging team members to support one another, can significantly impact workplace dynamics. Establishing kindness challenges or appreciation days can encourage employees to share positive feedback and express gratitude. These initiatives serve as reminders of the importance of fostering a culture rooted in respect and appreciation. As employees participate in these activities, they collectively reinforce the value of kindness, reducing the likelihood of gossip taking hold.

Moreover, embracing kindness can lead to increased productivity. When employees feel supported and appreciated, they are more likely to engage fully in their work and contribute positively to team goals. A culture of kindness minimizes distractions caused by negativity and gossip, allowing individuals to focus on their tasks and collaborate effectively. As morale improves, employees are happier and more motivated, leading to enhanced performance and creativity. This positive cycle not only benefits individuals but also contributes to the overall success of the organization.

Ultimately, embracing a culture of kindness is a proactive approach to breaking the cycle of workplace gossip. By prioritizing empathy, recognition, and supportive initiatives, organizations can create a thriving environment where employees feel safe and valued. This transformation begins with a commitment to kindness at every level, leading to improved morale, increased productivity, and a stronger sense of community within the workplace. By fostering a culture of kindness, organizations can pave the way for lasting change, ensuring that gossip is replaced with constructive dialogue and collaboration.

The Role of Emotional Intelligence

The Sound of Silence: Breaking the Cycle of Workplace Gossip

Emotional intelligence plays a pivotal role in navigating the complexities of workplace relationships, particularly in environments where gossip thrives. When employees possess a high level of emotional intelligence, they are better equipped to recognize and manage their own emotions, as well as those of their colleagues. This awareness fosters healthier interactions, allowing individuals to engage constructively rather than succumb to the negativity that often accompanies gossip. By developing emotional intelligence, employees can create a more supportive atmosphere, reducing the likelihood of misunderstandings and conflict.

Individuals with strong emotional intelligence are adept at empathizing with others. This ability to understand and share the feelings of colleagues can significantly mitigate the damaging effects of gossip. When team members feel heard and valued, they are less likely to resort to negative talk about one another. Instead, they are more inclined to address issues directly and respectfully. This promotes a culture of open communication, where challenges can be resolved collaboratively rather than through the whispers that can erode trust and morale.

Furthermore, emotional intelligence empowers individuals to manage their reactions in challenging situations. Instead of impulsively responding to gossip or engaging in it themselves, emotionally intelligent employees can pause and assess the implications of their words and actions. This self-regulation not only prevents the spread of harmful rumors but also sets a positive example for others. As more employees practice this restraint, the overall workplace culture begins to shift, leading to increased harmony and cooperation among team members.

The benefits of fostering emotional intelligence extend beyond individual interactions; they can have a profound impact on overall productivity and morale. A workplace characterized by emotional intelligence is often marked by higher levels of trust, collaboration, and engagement. When employees feel safe and respected, they are more likely to contribute their best work, leading to enhanced performance and innovation. By breaking the cycle of gossip through emotional intelligence, organizations can cultivate an environment where everyone thrives.

In conclusion, enhancing emotional intelligence within the workplace is a powerful strategy for combating gossip and its detrimental effects. By prioritizing emotional awareness, empathy, and self-regulation, employees can transform their interactions, fostering a culture of respect and positivity. This not only strengthens relationships but also boosts morale and productivity. As we embrace the principles of emotional intelligence, we pave the way for a more harmonious and successful workplace, breaking free from the cycle of gossip and nurturing a culture of support and collaboration.

Continuous Improvement and Adaptation

In the ever-evolving landscape of the workplace, continuous improvement and adaptation are essential components in breaking the cycle of gossip. Embracing change and fostering a culture of open communication can transform an environment plagued by negativity into one characterized by collaboration and positivity. By focusing on ongoing development, organizations can not only mitigate the effects of gossip but also enhance overall morale and productivity.

The Sound of Silence: Breaking the Cycle of Workplace Gossip

Establishing a framework for continuous improvement involves actively seeking feedback from employees at all levels. Encouraging team members to share their thoughts and experiences can unveil underlying issues that contribute to workplace gossip. When employees feel heard and valued, they are more likely to engage in meaningful conversations, reducing misunderstandings and fostering a sense of belonging. This collaborative atmosphere cultivates trust and transparency, which are crucial in dismantling the barriers that gossip often creates.

Adaptation plays a vital role in this process. As workplace dynamics shift, so must the strategies employed to combat gossip. Organizations should regularly assess their communication practices and be open to implementing new methods that resonate with their workforce. This could mean adopting more inclusive decision-making processes or utilizing technology to streamline communication. By staying attuned to the needs and preferences of employees, leaders can create an environment that not only discourages gossip but encourages constructive dialogue.

Moreover, continuous improvement is not just about addressing the existing issues; it's about fostering a proactive approach that anticipates potential challenges. Training programs focused on communication skills, conflict resolution, and emotional intelligence can equip employees with the tools they need to navigate difficult conversations. Empowering individuals to handle disputes before they escalate fosters a culture of respect and understanding, essential for minimizing gossip and its detrimental impacts on morale and productivity.

Ultimately, the journey toward breaking the cycle of workplace gossip hinges on a commitment to continuous improvement and adaptation. Leaders and employees alike must champion a culture of open dialogue, adaptability, and mutual respect. By embracing these principles, organizations can not only diminish the harmful effects of gossip but also cultivate a thriving workplace where collaboration and positivity flourish, leading to enhanced morale and productivity for everyone involved.

Chapter 9: Success Stories of Gossip-Free Workplaces

Learning from Companies that Thrived

In examining how companies have successfully thrived despite the pervasive challenge of workplace gossip, it becomes clear that a proactive approach can fundamentally transform an organization's culture. Companies that have flourished often prioritize open communication and transparency, creating environments where employees feel valued and heard. For instance, organizations that implement regular check-ins and feedback sessions foster a sense of belonging and trust among team members. By making space for honest dialogue, they not only diminish the likelihood of gossip but also enhance morale and productivity.

The Sound of Silence: Breaking the Cycle of Workplace Gossip

A notable example is a tech company that faced significant gossip challenges early in its development. Leadership recognized that unchecked rumors were negatively impacting team dynamics and overall effectiveness. They initiated a series of workshops focused on building a culture of respect and collaboration. These sessions empowered employees to voice concerns directly rather than resorting to whispers behind closed doors. As a result, the company witnessed a remarkable shift in employee engagement and a reduction in gossip-related tensions, ultimately leading to improved performance and innovation.

Similarly, organizations that encourage team-building activities create stronger bonds among employees, which can significantly reduce the prevalence of gossip. By investing in social events, retreats, and collaborative projects, companies foster relationships built on trust and mutual respect. This investment in interpersonal connections not only helps to combat the spread of rumors but also cultivates a more cohesive work environment. As employees grow to understand and appreciate one another, they become less likely to indulge in harmful gossip, recognizing its detrimental impact on their colleagues and the organization as a whole.

Moreover, companies that embrace a strong set of core values tend to have a lower incidence of gossip. When all employees are aligned with the same mission and ethical standards, there is a greater sense of accountability. Leaders play a crucial role in modeling these values, and when they demonstrate integrity and respect in their interactions, it sets a powerful example for everyone else. Employees are more inclined to follow suit, fostering a culture where gossip is not only discouraged but actively replaced with positive reinforcement and supportive communication.

Ultimately, learning from companies that have thrived in spite of workplace gossip reveals that taking proactive steps can create a harmonious and productive work environment. By prioritizing open communication, team-building, and strong values, organizations can significantly mitigate the harmful effects of gossip. With a commitment to fostering a culture of respect and collaboration, companies not only enhance employee morale but also unlock the full potential of their workforce. As the cycle of gossip is broken, a newfound sense of unity and purpose emerges, driving both individual and collective success.

Testimonials from Employees

The impact of workplace gossip can sometimes obscure the positive experiences employees have within their organizations. However, firsthand testimonials from employees reveal a different narrative, one that highlights resilience, camaraderie, and the importance of open communication. These stories offer valuable insights into how individuals navigate the challenges posed by gossip while fostering a supportive work environment.

One employee shared their journey of overcoming a challenging work culture that was once riddled with rumors and speculation. They described how, through open dialogues and team-building initiatives, the atmosphere shifted from one of distrust to a space where collaboration thrived. This transformation not only boosted morale but also ignited a renewed sense of purpose among colleagues. When employees feel safe to express their thoughts and feelings, it cultivates a culture where everyone can contribute positively.

The Sound of Silence: Breaking the Cycle of Workplace Gossip

Another employee recounted a particularly difficult period when gossip threatened to derail a major project. Instead of succumbing to negativity, the team rallied together, focusing on transparent communication and collective problem-solving. This approach not only quelled the rumors but also strengthened team bonds. The individual emphasized that such experiences taught them the value of unity and how addressing issues head-on can lead to greater success and fulfillment.

Additionally, many employees noted the role of supportive leadership in combating workplace gossip. They highlighted instances where managers took proactive measures to foster a positive environment, such as implementing regular check-ins and feedback sessions. These practices not only diminished the prevalence of gossip but also empowered employees to voice their concerns openly. This kind of leadership encourages a culture of trust, where individuals feel valued and heard, ultimately enhancing productivity and job satisfaction.

The testimonials of these employees remind us that while workplace gossip can have detrimental effects, it is possible to break the cycle through intentional actions and a commitment to fostering a positive environment. By leaning on each other, embracing open communication, and fostering a culture of support, employees can navigate the challenges of gossip and emerge stronger together. These stories serve as a beacon of hope, illustrating that a collaborative and respectful workplace is not just a dream but a tangible reality that can be achieved.

Strategies that Worked for Others

In the journey toward a healthier workplace environment, many organizations have successfully tackled the issue of gossip through innovative strategies. By learning from their experiences, you can find inspiration and practical solutions that may work for your own team. One effective approach has been the implementation of open communication channels. Organizations that prioritize transparency often see a significant reduction in gossip. When employees feel safe to share their thoughts and concerns directly with management, they are less likely to rely on informal, potentially damaging conversations. This fosters trust and strengthens relationships among colleagues, leading to a more unified workforce.

Another strategy that has proven beneficial is the establishment of clear policies regarding workplace behavior. Companies that have set explicit guidelines about gossip have empowered their employees to hold each other accountable. By defining what constitutes gossip and emphasizing the importance of respectful communication, these organizations create a culture where employees feel encouraged to address issues constructively rather than resorting to rumor-mongering. This not only helps in curbing negative conversations but also promotes a sense of ownership among team members, as they recognize their role in maintaining a positive work environment.

In addition to policies, training and workshops on effective communication can be transformative. Organizations that invest in their employees' interpersonal skills often witness a remarkable shift in workplace dynamics. These training sessions can equip staff with tools to engage in open dialogue, resolve conflicts amicably, and support one another. When employees learn to communicate effectively, they are less likely to engage in gossip. Instead, they become advocates for each other, fostering a culture of respect and collaboration that enhances overall morale and productivity.

The Sound of Silence: Breaking the Cycle of Workplace Gossip

Celebrating positive behavior is another strategy that has yielded impressive results. Organizations that highlight and reward employees for their contributions to a positive work culture create an environment where gossip is less likely to thrive. Recognition programs can take various forms, from shout-outs in team meetings to formal awards. By showcasing individuals who exemplify integrity and collaboration, companies motivate others to follow suit. This not only diminishes the appeal of gossip but also builds a community where employees feel valued and appreciated.

Finally, encouraging team-building activities can significantly reduce gossip in the workplace. When employees engage in collaborative projects or social events, they develop deeper connections with one another. These shared experiences foster empathy and understanding, making it more challenging for gossip to take root. Organizations that prioritize team cohesion often find that employees are more supportive of one another and less inclined to participate in negative talk. By investing in these relationships, you can cultivate an environment where positivity prevails, ultimately enhancing both morale and productivity.

Chapter 10: Conclusion: Building a Harmonious Workplace

Recap of Key Takeaways

In reflecting on the key takeaways from "The Sound of Silence: Breaking the Cycle of Workplace Gossip," it is essential to understand the profound impact that gossip can have on workplace dynamics. Workplace gossip often creates an environment filled with mistrust and negativity. When employees engage in gossip, it not only affects the individuals involved but also creates a ripple effect that can diminish morale across the entire organization. Recognizing these consequences is the first step toward fostering a healthier workplace culture.

One critical takeaway is the importance of open communication. Encouraging employees to express their thoughts and concerns in a constructive manner can significantly reduce the urge to resort to gossip. By creating platforms for dialogue, organizations empower their teams to share their ideas and feedback openly. This transparency fosters a sense of belonging and trust, which ultimately enhances morale and productivity. When employees feel heard and valued, they are less likely to engage in gossip and more likely to contribute positively to their work environment.

Another vital point is the role of leadership in modeling appropriate behavior. Leaders set the tone for workplace culture, and their actions speak louder than words. By demonstrating integrity, respect, and professionalism, leaders can discourage gossip and promote a culture of support and collaboration. When leadership actively works to eliminate gossip, it sends a clear message that such behavior is not tolerated. This commitment can lead to a more cohesive team that is focused on achieving common goals rather than engaging in divisive chatter.

The Sound of Silence: Breaking the Cycle of Workplace Gossip

Additionally, implementing team-building activities can play a significant role in reducing workplace gossip. These activities encourage collaboration and strengthen relationships among team members. When employees get to know each other better, they are less likely to misunderstand intentions and more likely to communicate directly. Building rapport among colleagues fosters an environment of respect and understanding, which diminishes the likelihood of gossip taking root. Investing in team-building initiatives is not just beneficial; it is a proactive approach to enhancing workplace morale.

Finally, it is crucial to cultivate a culture of accountability. Encouraging employees to take responsibility for their words and actions can deter gossip and promote a more positive atmosphere. When individuals recognize the power of their language and the impact it has on their colleagues, they are more likely to choose their words wisely. By establishing clear guidelines around communication and ensuring that everyone understands the consequences of gossip, organizations can create a more respectful and productive workplace. With these key takeaways in mind, it is possible to break the cycle of workplace gossip and build a thriving, harmonious environment.

The Ongoing Journey to a Gossip-Free Environment

Creating a gossip-free environment in the workplace is an ongoing journey that requires dedication, awareness, and collective effort. It begins with recognizing the negative impact gossip can have on morale and productivity. When employees engage in gossip, it often leads to misunderstandings, damaged relationships, and a toxic culture that stifles collaboration and creativity. By acknowledging these effects, organizations can take proactive steps to foster a more positive atmosphere where open communication and trust thrive.

To embark on this journey, leadership plays a crucial role in setting the tone. Leaders must model the behavior they wish to see in their teams by avoiding gossip themselves and promoting transparency. By encouraging open dialogue and creating safe spaces for employees to express their concerns, leaders can demonstrate that a culture of respect and support is paramount. This not only empowers employees but also establishes a foundation for a healthier workplace where everyone feels valued and heard.

Training and development programs can further support the goal of a gossip-free environment. Workshops focused on effective communication skills, conflict resolution, and emotional intelligence can equip employees with the tools they need to navigate interpersonal relationships more effectively. By investing in these resources, organizations signal their commitment to fostering a respectful workplace culture. When employees feel confident in their communication skills, they are less likely to resort to gossip as a means of addressing issues or frustrations.

Encouraging peer accountability is another vital component of this journey. Employees should feel empowered to hold one another accountable for their actions and to speak up when they witness gossip. This can be achieved through team-building activities that promote trust and strengthen relationships among colleagues. When a culture of mutual respect is cultivated, employees naturally become more invested in supporting one another and maintaining a positive environment. This peer support system can significantly reduce the prevalence of gossip and enhance overall workplace morale.

The Sound of Silence: Breaking the Cycle of Workplace Gossip

Ultimately, the ongoing journey to a gossip-free environment is about cultivating a culture of respect, openness, and collaboration. While the path may have its challenges, the rewards are immeasurable. Organizations that commit to this journey will not only see improvements in employee morale and productivity but will also foster a sense of belonging and purpose among their teams. By working together to break the cycle of workplace gossip, we can create a thriving environment where every individual can contribute their best selves, leading to greater success for everyone involved.

Encouragement to Take Action Today

In today's fast-paced work environment, it can be easy to overlook the impact of workplace gossip. Often dismissed as mere chatter, this behavior can significantly undermine morale and productivity. By recognizing the consequences of gossip, we empower ourselves to take action. Acknowledging that gossip creates a toxic atmosphere is the first step toward fostering a healthier workplace. It is time to step away from the sidelines and actively contribute to a culture of respect and collaboration.

Taking action against gossip begins with each individual. You have the power to influence your work environment positively. It starts with being mindful of your own words and actions. Instead of engaging in negative conversations, choose to uplift your colleagues and share constructive feedback. By setting this example, you can inspire others to follow suit, creating a ripple effect that promotes a more supportive workplace culture. Your commitment to positive communication can transform your team's dynamics significantly.

Moreover, consider addressing gossip when you encounter it. It can be daunting to confront a colleague about their behavior, but doing so is crucial for cultivating a respectful workplace. Approach the situation with empathy and understanding, and express how gossip can harm team cohesion and individual morale. This courageous step not only helps to halt the spread of negativity but also encourages others to reflect on their own participation in such discussions. By fostering an environment where open communication and honesty are valued, you contribute to a workplace that thrives on trust and mutual support.

Engaging in team-building activities is another effective way to combat workplace gossip. Organizing events that promote collaboration and connection can bridge gaps and foster a sense of belonging among colleagues. When team members develop stronger relationships, they are less likely to engage in harmful gossip. Strive to create opportunities for open dialogue, where everyone feels safe to share their ideas and concerns. By facilitating interactions that build trust, you play a pivotal role in shaping a positive workplace culture.

Finally, remember that change takes time, but every small action counts. By committing to break the cycle of workplace gossip today, you are contributing to a brighter future for your team and organization. Embrace the challenge of fostering a gossip-free environment, and encourage others to join you on this journey. Together, you can create a workplace where everyone feels valued, respected, and motivated to perform at their best. Let today be the day you take a stand against gossip and begin to cultivate a culture of positivity and productivity.